ARTIFICIAL INTELLIGENCE UNLEASHED

AN ENTREPRENEUR'S GUIDE TO INNOVATION

EMPOWERING SMALL BUSINESSES

KIMBERLY BURK CORDOVA

COPYRIGHT

Copyright © 2026 Thrive Collective

All rights reserved.

No part of this publication may be reproduced, stored in a retrieval system, or transmitted in any form or by any means, electronic, mechanical, photocopying, recording, scanning, or otherwise, without the prior written permission of the publisher, except as permitted by applicable copyright law.

For permissions, contact the publisher via https://www.ThriveCollectiveHQ.com

This publication is provided for informational and educational purposes only. While the author and publisher have made every effort to ensure the accuracy of the content, they make no representations or warranties regarding completeness, reliability, or suitability. The author and publisher shall not be liable for any losses, damages, or adverse outcomes arising from the use of this material.

Any URLs or external websites referenced are provided for convenience. The author and publisher are not responsible for the content, availability, or accuracy of external sites, and links may change over time.

All trademarks, service marks, trade names, and product names referenced in this publication are the property of their respective owners. Use of these names does not imply endorsement. The author and publisher are not affiliated with, sponsored by, or endorsed by any third-party companies mentioned.

The author asserts the moral right to be identified as the author of this work.

TABLE OF CONTENTS

Introduction	vii
1. Understanding AI and Its Business Applications	1
2. A Comprehensive Guide to Assessing AI Readiness and Opportunities in Your Business	5
3. Developing an AI Strategy for Small Businesses	11
4. Data Preparation and Collection	15
5. Choosing the Best AI Solution for Your Business	19
6. Implementing AI in Your Business	23
7. Maximizing AI Performance *Measuring Success and ROI*	29
8. Overcoming Challenges and Pitfalls	33
9. Case Studies and Success Stories	37
10. Looking Ahead *Future Trends in AI for Small Business*	43
11. Ethical Considerations and Responsible AI Practices	47
12. Practical Applications Across Industries	51
13. Scaling Up *Deploying AI Solutions*	55
Conclusion	61
Appendix	65
Appendix	69
Appendix	73
Appendix	77
A Quick Favor	81
About Kimberly Burk Cordova	83
Join Our Mailing List	85
Also by Thrive Collective	87
Bibliography	91

INTRODUCTION

Unlocking the Power of Artificial Intelligence for Small Businesses

In today's fast-paced business landscape, artificial intelligence (AI) is a beacon of hope, offering practical benefits that can boost your small business. Consider a local boutique, much like yours, that once grappled with the inventory management challenge. Three years ago, they bravely ventured into AI, not with a complex system, but with a simple yet powerful tool-a demand forecasting algorithm. This practical approach to AI optimization led to a resounding success. They slashed inventory waste by an impressive 40% and saw sales soar by 25%. This isn't just a success story; it's a testament to how AI can deliver real, tangible results for small businesses like yours, inspiring confidence in your own journey.

My journey into AI didn't start in a lab but in entrepreneurial workshops, where digital transformation was the buzz. Initially, AI seemed distant, reserved for the tech elite. Fueled by a desire to bridge this gap, I embarked on a mission: to make AI approachable and actionable for entrepreneurs like you. This guide isn't just a theoretical discourse; it's a practical roadmap meticulously crafted to demystify AI for those without a tech background. With clear explanations and step-by-step guidance, it

Introduction

equips you with the knowledge and tools to confidently integrate AI into your business operations, empowering you to take charge of your digital transformation. After reading this guide, you will feel confident and prepared to start your AI journey.

AI can seem daunting, wrapped in technical complexity. Yet, this book aims to dismantle those barriers, serving as your bridge to understanding and applying AI, regardless of your business's size. Real-world case studies, success stories, and practical tips illuminate the path from theory to practice.

Moreover, as we embrace this technological transformation, we must navigate its ethical landscape. This guide doesn't shy away from the tough questions about privacy, fairness, and transparency. It emphasizes the importance of adopting AI responsibly and ethically, so you can trust that your AI integration aligns with your values. We delve into topics such as data privacy, algorithmic bias, and the ethical use of AI in decision-making, providing you with a holistic understanding of the ethical implications of AI. By being aware of these considerations, you can confidently and responsibly incorporate AI into your business, fostering trust with your customers and stakeholders.

If you're reading this, you're eager to leverage AI to enhance your small business operations, overcome market competition, and achieve growth without high costs or resources. This guidebook addresses these aspirations and challenges head-on by highlighting affordable and scalable AI solutions tailored to small businesses, from retail stores to service providers like yours. It aims to show you that AI adoption is possible even with limited budgets and resources, helping you take confident steps toward digital transformation.

So, I invite you to join me with an open mind and a readiness to experiment. Consider this book not just a read but your companion in the exciting journey of AI integration. It's filled with informed insights, encouragement, and actionable advice, and also includes interactive exercises and case studies to help you apply the concepts to your business.

As we embark on this journey into AI, let's remember the immense opportunities it presents. With the right tools and knowledge, the future is bright for entrepreneurs and small businesses. However, it's essential to know the potential risks and challenges, such as data security and algorithmic bias. AI isn't just a survival tool; it's a catalyst for your business to thrive and compete on a new level. Let's embrace this transformative journey together, filled with excitement and optimism for what lies ahead.

ONE

UNDERSTANDING AI AND ITS BUSINESS APPLICATIONS

AI Fundamentals

In today's rapidly evolving business landscape, understanding the transformative potential of artificial intelligence (AI) is crucial for entrepreneurs and small businesses looking to stay ahead of the curve. AI has the power to revolutionize industries and completely transform the way we do business, making it not just essential but an exciting opportunity for business owners to familiarize themselves with its basic principles and applications.

One of the key AI fundamentals that entrepreneurs should be aware of is machine learning. Machine learning is a subset of AI that enables machines to learn from data and improve performance without being explicitly programmed. This technology can analyze large amounts of data, identify patterns, and make predictions. For instance, a retail business can use machine learning to analyze customer data and predict future buying patterns, thereby optimizing its inventory and sales strategies. This demonstrates how AI can streamline processes, maximize decision-making, and enhance customer experiences.

Another essential concept in AI fundamentals is natural language processing (NLP). NLP is a branch of AI that enables machines to understand, interpret, and generate human language. This technology is used in chatbots, virtual assistants, and language translation services, allowing businesses to automate customer interactions, personalize marketing campaigns, and improve communication with clients and employees.

Entrepreneurs should also be familiar with computer vision, an AI field that enables machines to interpret and understand visual information from the world around them. Computer vision is used in facial recognition, autonomous vehicles, and medical imaging, allowing businesses to automate tasks, enhance security measures, and improve product quality through visual inspection.

Lastly, entrepreneurs should understand the importance of data quality and ethics in AI. Data quality is crucial for the success of AI systems, as inaccurate or biased data can lead to flawed results and decision-making. Additionally, ethical considerations such as privacy, transparency, and accountability should be taken into account when implementing AI technologies to ensure businesses use them responsibly and ethically. However, it's important to note that implementing AI also entails challenges and risks, including the need for skilled personnel and the potential for job displacement. By mastering these AI fundamentals and understanding these challenges, entrepreneurs and small businesses can harness the power of AI to drive innovation, improve efficiency, and gain a competitive edge in today's digital economy.

AI in Business

AI has become a game-changer for businesses of all sizes, offering practical solutions to streamline operations, increase productivity, and drive growth. In today's competitive market, small business owners have a unique opportunity to embrace AI technology to stay ahead of the curve, transform their business, and feel empowered to succeed. From automated customer service chatbots to predictive analytics tools, AI presents a wealth of opportunities for entrepreneurs to enhance their business processes and make informed decisions.

One key benefit of incorporating AI into business operations is its ability to automate repetitive tasks, freeing up valuable time and resources for small business owners to focus on strategic initiatives. For example, AI-powered software can analyze large volumes of data in real-time, identify patterns, and generate insights to help businesses make more informed decisions. This level of automation improves operational efficiency and enables enterprises to deliver a more personalized and responsive customer experience.

AI also plays a crucial role in enhancing customer engagement and satisfaction. By leveraging AI-powered chatbots, businesses can provide round-the-clock customer support, address inquiries promptly, and deliver tailored recommendations based on individual preferences. This level of personalized interaction fosters customer loyalty and helps businesses better understand their target audience and anticipate their needs.

Moreover, AI can help small businesses unlock new revenue streams by identifying untapped market opportunities and predicting future trends. Through predictive analytics, companies can analyze historical data, identify patterns, and forecast future outcomes with high accuracy. This enables small business owners to make informed decisions about product development, marketing strategies, and resource allocation, ultimately driving business growth and profitability.

In conclusion, when harnessed by entrepreneurs, AI is a powerful tool that can revolutionize how small businesses operate and compete in today's fast-paced digital economy. By embracing AI technology, entrepreneurs can streamline operations, enhance customer engagement, and drive growth in previously unimaginable ways. As the business landscape evolves, small business owners can adapt and leverage AI to stay ahead of the curve and remain competitive in their industries.

TWO

A COMPREHENSIVE GUIDE TO ASSESSING AI READINESS AND OPPORTUNITIES IN YOUR BUSINESS

Introduction

Before embarking on the journey of artificial intelligence (AI), entrepreneurs and small businesses should envision the potential benefits that AI can bring to their unique business needs and goals. AI, a powerful tool, has the potential to streamline processes, elevate customer experiences, and revolutionize decision-making. While not every business may benefit from adopting AI technology, this chapter offers a comprehensive approach to understanding and adopting AI, combining readiness assessment with identifying AI opportunities. This can help entrepreneurs feel more confident about making informed choices.

Evaluating Your Business Needs

The first crucial step in assessing AI readiness is to deeply understand your business needs. This involves determining whether AI aligns with your business goals and whether it can add significant value to your operations. Your unique business needs are not just a part of this process; they are the heart of it, making your role in this assessment invaluable. Recognizing this can help entrepreneurs feel more in control and prepared for the next steps.

Complexity of Operations

AI is best suited for businesses with large volumes of data and complex processes that can benefit from automation and data analysis. For instance, a manufacturing company with intricate supply chain operations could leverage AI to optimize inventory management. However, AI may not be necessary if your business primarily deals with simple tasks or has minimal data. Small retail stores, for example, should consider whether their operations can benefit from AI, and explore lightweight solutions or phased approaches to address concerns about applicability.

Target Audience

Consider your target audience and market. AI can enhance customer experiences through personalized recommendations, chatbots, and predictive analytics. AI could be a valuable asset if your audience values highly customized experiences.

Technological Infrastructure

Assess your current technological infrastructure. Do your systems and processes support AI technology? Ensure you have the necessary hardware and software to support AI implementation.

Team Readiness

Evaluate your team's readiness for AI adoption. Do your employees have the necessary skills and knowledge? Are they open to learning new tools and techniques? Providing training and support is crucial for a successful transition.

Data Quality and Availability

AI relies heavily on data for informed decision-making. Ensure you have clean, accurate, and relevant data. Review your data sources to confirm they are reliable and up to date.

Business Impact

Consider the potential impact of AI on your operations. How will it improve efficiency, productivity, and customer satisfaction? Identify potential risks and challenges associated with AI implementation.

Identifying Business Needs and Challenges

Understanding your business's specific needs and challenges is critical to effective AI implementation. This involves identifying areas where AI can make a significant difference, guiding you towards the most impactful use of AI in your operations.

Streamlining Processes

AI can help automate repetitive tasks, analyze data faster, and improve decision-making. Identify areas in your operations where efficiency can be improved.

Industry Trends and Market Demands

Stay informed about industry trends and market demands that impact your business. For instance, companies in natural language processing (NLP) or computer vision may require AI solutions to enhance their offerings.

Fraud Detection and Cybersecurity

With the rise of cyber threats, implementing AI for fraud detection and cybersecurity is essential. AI can help detect and prevent fraudulent activity in real time.

Real-World Case Studies of Successful AI Implementations

Learning from real-world examples can provide invaluable insights into the successful implementation of AI across various industries. These examples are not just beacons of inspiration; they are also a testament to the transformative power of AI, instilling confidence in its potential benefits and reassuring you of its effectiveness. Seeing tangible results can help entrepreneurs feel more assured about AI's capabilities.

E-Commerce Startup

An e-commerce startup used machine learning algorithms to personalize product recommendations, increasing sales and customer retention by analyzing browsing history, purchase behavior, and demographic data.

Financial Sector

A brokerage firm implemented AI-powered trading algorithms to automate investment decisions. The algorithms made real-time trading decisions by analyzing market trends and historical data, resulting in higher profits and reduced risk.

Healthcare Industry

A hospital uses an NLP system to analyze medical records and identify patterns to improve patient outcomes. This AI system helps doctors make more informed diagnoses and treatment decisions.

Cybersecurity

A technology company used AI-powered fraud-detection algorithms to identify and prevent fraudulent activity. The AI system analyzes user behavior and transaction patterns in real time, protecting the company from financial losses and security threats.

Quick Wins and Low-Hanging Fruit for Immediate Impact

Entrepreneurs and small business owners must find quick wins that can immediately impact their bottom line when implementing AI.

Natural Language Processing (NLP)

Implement NLP to automate customer service inquiries, analyze customer feedback, and create personalized marketing campaigns.

Computer Vision and Image Recognition

Use computer vision for quality control inspections, facial recognition for security, and interactive customer experiences.

Fraud Detection and Cybersecurity

Leverage AI algorithms to detect and prevent fraudulent activities and monitor cybersecurity threats.

Personalized Marketing and Recommendation Systems

Analyze customer data and behavior to create customized marketing campaigns and product recommendations, increasing customer engagement and sales.

Readiness Checklist

To ensure successful AI implementation, use this readiness checklist:

1. **Evaluate Technology Infrastructure:** Assess compatibility with AI and identify hardware and software gaps.
2. **Team Readiness:** Ensure your team has the necessary skills and is open to learning new tools.
3. **Data Quality:** Confirm the availability of clean, accurate, and relevant data.
4. **Impact Assessment:** Understand how AI will improve efficiency and customer satisfaction and identify potential risks.
5. **Implementation Plan:** Define goals, timeline, and budget for AI integration. Consider working with AI experts or consultants.

Conclusion

Adopting AI is a strategic move that requires a 'holistic approach '. This approach involves evaluating your business needs, identifying specific opportunities, assessing your readiness, developing an implementation plan, and considering the ethical implications of AI adoption. By following this comprehensive approach, you can ensure that AI adds tangible value to your business. Use the readiness checklist to guide your preparations and ensure a successful AI implementation. This holistic approach, encompassing all aspects of AI adoption, will help you stay competitive in today's rapidly evolving business landscape.

THREE

DEVELOPING AN AI STRATEGY FOR SMALL BUSINESSES

Integrating artificial intelligence (AI) into small business operations can be a game-changer in today's competitive market. However, developing a comprehensive AI strategy requires careful planning and execution. This guide will provide a detailed, step-by-step approach to creating an AI strategy tailored to your business needs.

Understanding Your Business Objectives

- **Start by defining clear, specific goals:** as this helps you feel confident and motivated, knowing your AI efforts are purposeful and aligned with your business needs.

Setting Clear Goals and Objectives

- **Make your goals measurable and realistic:** Instead of vague objectives like "improve customer experience," set specific targets like "reduce customer wait times by 20%." This clarity will help you track progress and make informed decisions about your AI implementation.

Assessing AI Readiness

- **Evaluate your current technological infrastructure:** Assess whether your systems and processes are compatible with AI technology. Identify gaps or areas needing improvement before moving forward with AI integration.

Budgeting and Resource Allocation

- **Assess your current resources:** evaluate your team members' skills and expertise, and the hardware and software you already have. Determine what additional resources are needed to support AI implementation.
- **Allocate a budget for AI implementation:** Consider the costs of acquiring new technology, hiring skilled employees, and providing necessary training. Prioritize investments with the most significant impact on achieving your business goals.

Understanding Data Infrastructure

- **Evaluate your current technological infrastructure:** by examining the quality, accuracy, and accessibility of your data, ensuring your data collection and management systems support practical AI analysis and decision-making.

Prioritizing Use Cases

- **Identify impactful and feasible use cases:** by considering how AI can address your specific challenges, such as customer service or inventory management, ensure your focus aligns with your business needs and resources.

Building a Cross-Functional Team

- **Create a diverse, skilled team:** Bring together individuals from diverse backgrounds and disciplines to ensure your team has the knowledge and expertise to tackle complex AI projects; Foster collaboration and communication among team members to drive innovation and creativity.

Creating a Roadmap for Implementation

- **Develop a detailed implementation plan:** That Outlines the specific AI technologies you will use, the implementation timeline, and the resources needed to support your initiatives. Break down your plan into smaller, manageable tasks to ensure each step is completed on time and within budget.
- **Involve key stakeholders in the planning process:** to help you feel supported and confident, knowing your AI initiatives have organizational backing and shared understanding.

Continuous Monitoring and Evaluation

- **Track critical metrics and KPIs:** to give you a sense of control and reassurance, ensuring your AI initiatives are on track and delivering tangible results.
- **Stay informed about the latest AI trends:** Keep up to date with the latest developments in AI technology and trends to continue innovating and stay ahead of the competition.

By following these steps and creating a comprehensive AI strategy tailored to your business, you can unlock artificial intelligence's full potential and drive innovation and growth in your organization. Remember to approach AI implementation thoughtfully and strategically, ensuring it adds tangible value to your business and helps you stay competitive in today's rapidly evolving business landscape.

FOUR

DATA PREPARATION AND COLLECTION

Importance of Quality Data

In today's fast-paced business environment, data is the lifeblood of any successful enterprise. Highlighting the importance of quality data can help entrepreneurs feel more confident in their AI initiatives, knowing they are building on a strong foundation.

When implementing AI in your business, the quality of the data you feed into your algorithms is crucial. For instance, a retail company that uses AI for demand forecasting relies on accurate sales data to make informed inventory decisions. Poor quality data in this case could lead to overstocking or understocking, both of which can be detrimental to the business. Similarly, a healthcare provider that uses AI for patient diagnosis needs high-quality medical data to ensure accurate results. Entrepreneurs and small companies must prioritize collecting, storing, and analyzing high-quality data to ensure the success of their AI projects. By doing so, they can harness the full potential of AI technologies such as machine learning, natural language processing, computer vision, and fraud detection.

Quality data is also essential for personalized marketing and recommendation systems. Businesses can effectively leverage customer data to tailor marketing campaigns to individual preferences, resulting in higher engagement and conversion rates. Additionally, sentiment analysis and social media monitoring rely on accurate data to understand customer behavior, sentiment, and trends. Without quality data, businesses risk missing valuable insights that can inform their marketing strategies and improve customer satisfaction.

In cybersecurity, high-quality data is critical for detecting and preventing fraudulent activity. By analyzing data patterns and anomalies, businesses can identify potential security threats and take proactive measures to protect their assets and sensitive information. Similarly, in financial trading algorithms, the accuracy and reliability of data are paramount in making informed investment decisions and maximizing returns.

In conclusion, the importance of quality data cannot be overstated when implementing AI technologies in business. Entrepreneurs and small companies must prioritize collecting, storing, and analyzing high-quality data to drive growth, innovation, and competitive advantage. By harnessing AI in areas such as personalized marketing, fraud detection, cybersecurity, and financial trading, businesses can unlock new opportunities, streamline operations, and stay ahead of the curve in today's digital economy. This not only ensures the success of your business but also paves the way for a more efficient and innovative future.

Data Privacy and Security Considerations

Data privacy and security considerations are crucial when implementing artificial intelligence (AI) in your business. As an entrepreneur or small business owner, understanding regulations such as GDPR and CCPA helps you navigate compliance risks. These can include data breaches, unauthorized access to sensitive information, and the potential for AI systems to make biased decisions. This subchapter explores key considerations to protect your data and ensure the security of your AI systems.

One of the main concerns regarding data privacy and security in AI is the risk of unauthorized access to sensitive information. Implementing standard security measures, such as encryption, access controls, and regular security audits, is essential to prevent unauthorized access to your data. Additionally, regular security audits and updates are necessary to stay ahead of potential threats and vulnerabilities.

Another important consideration is the ethical use of AI technology. Emphasizing transparency and fairness can help entrepreneurs feel reassured that their AI systems will be trustworthy and compliant, fostering confidence in their responsible use.

In addition to data privacy and ethical considerations, entrepreneurs and small businesses must also prioritize cybersecurity when implementing AI technology. Cyber attacks are becoming increasingly sophisticated, and AI systems can be vulnerable to hacking and malicious activities. Investing in cybersecurity measures, such as firewalls, intrusion detection systems, regular employee security training, and data encryption, is essential to protect your AI systems.

Data privacy and security considerations are essential for any business implementing AI technology. Stressing proactive measures such as encryption and regular audits can empower entrepreneurs to protect their data and AI systems effectively.

Leveraging Existing Data and Collecting New Data

In today's digital age, data is king. Entrepreneurs and small businesses have access to a wealth of data that can be leveraged to drive business growth and innovation. By combining existing data with new data collection strategies, companies can harness the power of artificial intelligence (AI) to make smarter decisions and improve their bottom line. This enhances your business's efficiency and gives you the confidence to make informed decisions that can lead to significant growth and success.

One key benefit of leveraging existing data is that it can provide valuable insights into customer behavior, market trends, and operational efficiency. By analyzing historical data, businesses can identify patterns and trends to inform more informed decisions about product development, marketing strategies, and customer engagement. This can lead to increased revenue, improved customer satisfaction, and a competitive edge in the marketplace.

In addition to leveraging existing data, collecting new data is essential for businesses implementing AI solutions. New data can provide fresh insights into changing consumer preferences, emerging market trends, and evolving industry dynamics. By collecting data from various sources, businesses can gain a more comprehensive understanding of their target audience and market landscape, enabling them to tailor their products and services to meet customer needs better.

When it comes to AI applications, data is the system's lifeblood. Whether businesses are looking to implement natural language processing (NLP) for customer service, computer vision for image recognition, or fraud detection for cybersecurity, having access to high-quality data is essential for the success of these initiatives. By combining existing data with new data-collection strategies, businesses can ensure their AI systems are trained on the most relevant and up-to-date information, leading to more accurate and reliable results.

Overall, leveraging existing data and collecting new data are essential to implementing AI in business. By combining the power of AI with a robust data strategy, entrepreneurs and small businesses can unlock new opportunities for growth, innovation, and success in today's competitive marketplace. By understanding the importance of data in AI applications, companies can take their operations to the next level and stay ahead of the curve in an ever-evolving digital landscape.

FIVE

CHOOSING THE BEST AI SOLUTION FOR YOUR BUSINESS

In the rapidly evolving landscape of artificial intelligence (AI), the potential for driving innovation, enhancing efficiency, and staying competitive is immense. This comprehensive guide will not only help you understand the different AI technologies but also ignite your excitement about the transformative power of AI in your business, inspiring you to explore new possibilities.

Understanding Different AI Models and Technologies

Before embarking on the selection process, it's paramount to grasp the various AI models and technologies available and their potential applications. AI encompasses many technologies, such as Machine Learning, Natural Language Processing (NLP), Computer Vision, and more. These technologies boast unique capabilities and can effectively address specific business challenges.

Machine Learning

Machine Learning enables computers to learn from data and make predictions or decisions without being explicitly programmed. It's widely used in the finance, healthcare, and marketing industries to analyze large datasets and extract valuable insights. Businesses can automate processes, optimize workflows, and improve decision-making by implementing machine learning algorithms.

Natural Language Processing (NLP)

NLP enables computers to understand, interpret, and generate human language. It's utilized in chatbots, virtual assistants, and sentiment analysis tools to automate customer service, analyze feedback, and personalize marketing campaigns. Leveraging NLP technologies can enhance customer interactions, improve communication, and gain a competitive edge.

Computer Vision

Computer Vision enables computers to interpret and understand visual information from the real world. It's employed in facial recognition systems, autonomous vehicles, and object detection tools to enhance safety, security, and efficiency. Integrating computer vision technologies into operations can streamline processes, boost productivity, and deliver innovative products and services.

Assessing Business Goals and Objectives

Understanding different AI technologies is just the beginning. The real power lies in aligning these technologies with your specific business goals and objectives. By defining clear goals, you can guide your AI implementation process and ensure every step supports your strategic vision.

Evaluating Solutions and Platforms

When evaluating AI solutions and platforms, consider factors such as use case, scalability, expertise, security, and compliance. Start by identifying the specific problem you're trying to solve and choosing a solution that aligns with your business objectives. Look for platforms that offer scalable options easily integrated with existing systems. Additionally, assess the AI solution provider's expertise and support to ensure a successful implementation.

Selecting Tools Aligned with Business Goals

Ensuring that AI tools align with your business goals is a pivotal step to realizing the full benefits of AI technology. It's crucial to identify your goals from the outset and evaluate the capabilities of the available AI tools. Consider factors such as accuracy, scalability, ease of integration, and cost. Moreover, consider your industry's specific needs and challenges when selecting tools tailored to your business niche.

Evaluating Vendors

Another critical aspect of implementing AI solutions is the thorough evaluation of vendors. It's essential to consider the vendor's track record, reputation, technical capabilities, pricing models, and level of customer support. Choosing a vendor with strong support can help you feel more secure and confident in your implementation journey.

Real-World Case Studies

Real-world case studies are not just examples; they are sources of inspiration and confidence. They show how AI solutions have driven innovation, enhanced efficiency, and achieved tangible results for businesses like yours. By learning from these success stories, you can confidently adapt strategies to your company and unlock the full potential of artificial intelligence.

Conclusion

Choosing the best AI solution for your business requires a thorough understanding of different AI technologies, alignment with business goals, evaluation of solutions and platforms, selection of tools, and assessment of vendors. By following this comprehensive approach and learning from real-world case studies, you can successfully implement AI technology to drive innovation, efficiency, and growth in your business, positioning yourself for success in today's competitive landscape.

SIX

IMPLEMENTING AI IN YOUR BUSINESS

In today's rapidly evolving business landscape, implementing artificial intelligence (AI) has become essential for your organization to stay competitive and drive innovation. This chapter will provide a comprehensive guide to effectively implementing AI in your business, covering key aspects such as developing AI models, integrating AI into existing processes, managing change, and training employees for AI adoption. By following these steps, you can harness the power of AI to enhance efficiency, improve decision-making, and unlock new opportunities for growth and success. The potential benefits of AI implementation are vast, from automating repetitive tasks and improving customer service to enabling more accurate and timely decision-making and unlocking new business opportunities.

Developing AI Models and Algorithms

The first step in implementing AI in your business is to develop AI models and algorithms tailored to your specific objectives. This involves identifying the problem you want to solve and gathering the necessary data to train your AI model. Whether improving customer service with chatbots, detecting fraudulent transactions, or analyzing text data for insights, clearly defining your objectives is crucial.

Once you have identified your objectives, it's time to choose a suitable algorithm for your problem. There are many different algorithms available, each with its strengths and weaknesses. For example, if you're working on sentiment analysis for social media monitoring, you may want to use a Recurrent Neural Network (RNN) or a Long Short-Term Memory (LSTM) model. These models are particularly effective in understanding the context and sentiment of social media posts. On the other hand, if you're developing a recommendation system for personalized marketing, a Collaborative Filtering algorithm might be more suitable. This algorithm analyzes user preferences and makes personalized recommendations.

After selecting the appropriate algorithm, the next step is to train your AI model. This involves feeding your data into the algorithm and adjusting its parameters until it can accurately predict outcomes. This process may require several iterations as you fine-tune your model to achieve the desired level of accuracy. Once trained, you can test your model on new data to evaluate its performance and make necessary adjustments.

Integrating AI into Existing Processes

Integrating AI into your existing processes is essential for realizing its full potential and driving business impact. For instance, in the healthcare industry, AI-powered diagnosis systems have significantly improved the accuracy and speed of disease detection. In the retail sector, AI-driven demand forecasting has helped businesses optimize their inventory management. Whether natural language processing (NLP) for communication, computer vision for image recognition, or fraud detection for cybersecurity, AI can enhance efficiency, accuracy, and scalability across various business domains.

One key aspect of integrating AI is assessing your current data and technology infrastructure. Ensure that your data is clean, organized, and easily accessible, as this will be crucial for training AI algorithms and extracting valuable insights. When selecting the right AI solution, consider factors such as the complexity of your problem, the availability of data, and the resources and expertise required for implementation.

Whether you choose a pre-built AI solution or develop a custom one, ensure it aligns with your objectives and is compatible with your existing systems. It's also important to consider the long-term implications of your AI solution, including scalability and adaptability to future needs.

Developing a comprehensive implementation plan is another critical step in integrating AI into your business. This plan should outline specific steps, including data preparation, algorithm training, testing, and deployment. By creating a clear, detailed plan, you can be assured that the implementation process will be smooth and efficient, reducing uncertainty and building confidence in your AI project.

Monitoring and evaluating your AI solution's performance is essential for continuous improvement and optimization. Regularly track key performance metrics such as accuracy, speed, and ROI to assess success. Gather end-user feedback to understand how the AI solution is being used and whether it's meeting their needs. This feedback can help you identify areas for improvement and make necessary adjustments to ensure ongoing value and alignment with your business objectives.

Change Management

Change management is crucial for successfully integrating AI into business operations. Managing resistance within your organization is essential for fostering a culture of innovation and ensuring the successful adoption of AI technologies. Strategies such as transparent communication, involving employees early, and demonstrating AI's benefits can help build support and reduce resistance.

Communicate openly and transparently with your team about the benefits of AI and how it will enhance their work rather than replace it. Your employees are the backbone of your business, and involving them in decision-making can foster trust and confidence. Provide training and support to alleviate their concerns and build their confidence in AI tools, making them feel valued and integral to your organization's AI journey.

Set clear goals and expectations for integrating AI technologies, focusing on areas significantly impacting your business. Regularly evaluate progress towards these goals and make adjustments to ensure a successful AI implementation.

Consider AI's impact on your existing processes and workflows, and develop a plan to address potential challenges such as data privacy, bias, and resistance. While AI can bring significant benefits, it also poses risks, including security concerns and algorithmic bias. Proactively addressing these issues, along with organizational changes, job roles, and communication channels, can help minimize disruptions and ensure a smooth transition to a more technologically advanced business model.

Training and Upskilling

Investing in employee training and upskilling is essential to maximizing the benefits of AI adoption and driving long-term success. Equip your employees with the necessary knowledge and skills to use AI tools effectively, streamline processes, and confidently make data-driven decisions.

Provide hands-on training opportunities for employees to practice using AI tools and software in real-world scenarios. Set up simulations or test environments where employees can experiment with AI algorithms and see how they can be applied to solve practical business problems.

Teach employees how to interpret and analyze the results generated by AI systems, including understanding how to interpret data outputs, troubleshoot errors, and make informed decisions based on AI recommendations. By providing employees with the skills to analyze AI-generated insights effectively, they will be better equipped to leverage the full potential of these technologies in their work.

Encourage a culture of continuous learning and improvement within your organization. This will foster innovation and competitiveness in the rapidly evolving business landscape. Investing in your employees' skills and knowledge can drive productivity, innovation, and success in today's AI-powered world.

In conclusion, implementing AI in your business may seem daunting, but with careful planning, strategic decision-making, and effective execution, it is entirely feasible. By following the steps outlined in this chapter, including developing AI models and algorithms, integrating AI into existing processes, managing change, and training employees for AI adoption, you can harness the power of AI to drive innovation, efficiency, and growth in your business. Embrace change, invest in your employees, and stay ahead of the curve to unlock new opportunities and achieve sustainable success in the digital age.

SEVEN

MAXIMIZING AI PERFORMANCE
MEASURING SUCCESS AND ROI

In the dynamic realm of artificial intelligence (AI), small businesses are increasingly leveraging AI technologies to foster innovation, streamline operations, and gain a competitive edge. This chapter aims to empower entrepreneurs with clear strategies, helping them feel confident in measuring AI success, tracking KPIs, and understanding ROI, which is essential for their growth and resilience.

Defining Key Performance Indicators (KPIs)

Key performance indicators (KPIs) are crucial metrics that enable businesses to make informed decisions by assessing AI effectiveness and impact across various domains. To ensure KPIs are meaningful, entrepreneurs should select metrics aligned with their specific AI applications, such as sentiment analysis accuracy for NLP or object detection accuracy for computer vision. For instance, in natural language processing (NLP) applications, KPIs such as sentiment analysis accuracy (measured by the percentage of correctly identified sentiments in a given text) and language model perplexity (measured by the average uncertainty of a language model in predicting the next word in a sequence) can help gauge the effectiveness of NLP algorithms. Similarly, in computer vision and image recognition, KPIs such as object detection accuracy (the percentage of correctly identified objects in an image) and image classification precision (the percentage of correctly classified images) are essential for evaluating AI model performance.

KPIs are critical in measuring AI success in fraud detection, cybersecurity, personalized marketing, sentiment analysis, robotics, and automation. By identifying and tracking relevant KPIs aligned with specific business goals, entrepreneurs can feel supported and confident in making data-driven decisions to optimize strategies.

Monitoring and Analyzing AI Performance

Monitoring AI performance involves tracking KPIs, analyzing data trends, and regularly testing and validating AI models. By closely tracking KPIs related to accuracy, efficiency, cost savings, and customer satisfaction, businesses can identify areas for improvement and optimize AI systems for better performance. This process helps entrepreneurs see how KPI tracking leads to tangible system improvements and fosters confidence in their AI management.

Regular testing and validation are essential to ensure the reliability and robustness of AI systems, particularly in applications such as financial trading algorithms and smart home technology. By conducting tests in different scenarios and environments, businesses can feel reassured that potential issues are addressed proactively, fostering trust in their AI solutions.

Calculating Return on Investment (ROI)

Calculating ROI for AI projects is essential for evaluating their financial impact and long-term viability. To make this more straightforward, outline the steps: compare the costs of implementing and maintaining AI projects, including initial investment, operational costs, and maintenance fees, with the benefits, such as cost savings, revenue, and scalability. Dividing net profit by total investment and expressing it as a percentage helps entrepreneurs see the direct link between investment and returns.

For example, implementing AI-powered fraud detection systems can lead to significant cost savings by reducing the risk of financial losses from fraud. Similarly, personalized marketing and recommendation systems can drive revenue growth by delivering targeted campaigns that boost sales and customer retention. By evaluating AI projects' short-term and long-term benefits, entrepreneurs can make informed decisions about resource allocation and prioritize investments with the highest ROI.

Iterating and Improving AI Strategies

Continuous iteration and improvement are not just essential; they are the key to unlocking the full potential of AI strategies and driving innovation in small businesses. Entrepreneurs can refine AI algorithms and enhance their performance over time by collecting and analyzing data, conducting testing and experimentation, and fostering collaboration within teams. This iterative approach not only keeps businesses ahead of the curve but also inspires a sense of progress and development, enabling them to adapt to new advancements in AI technology.

Ethical Considerations

In addition to measuring success, optimizing performance, and calculating ROI, ethical considerations are fundamental to responsible AI deployment. Entrepreneurs must prioritize fairness, transparency, and accountability in their AI strategies to mitigate potential risks and foster trust. This includes addressing issues such as bias in AI algorithms, privacy, data security, and the impact on employees and society. Emphasizing these points helps entrepreneurs understand that ethical practices are essential for responsible and trustworthy AI implementation and long-term success.

In conclusion, effectively measuring success, optimizing performance, and evaluating ROI are essential to successful AI implementation in small businesses. By defining relevant KPIs, monitoring AI performance, calculating ROI, iterating and improving AI strategies, and addressing ethical considerations, entrepreneurs can harness AI's full potential to drive innovation, improve efficiency, and achieve sustainable growth in today's digital economy.

EIGHT

OVERCOMING CHALLENGES AND PITFALLS

Addressing Ethical and Bias Concerns

As entrepreneurs and small businesses explore artificial intelligence (AI), addressing ethical and bias concerns is essential to build trust and demonstrate responsibility when implementing AI technologies. While AI has the potential to revolutionize industries and improve efficiency, it also has moral implications that must be carefully considered.

One of the key ethical concerns in AI is bias. AI systems are only as unbiased as the data they are trained on, and if that data is skewed or incomplete, it can lead to biased outcomes. This is particularly problematic in natural language processing (NLP) and computer vision, where bias can manifest as discriminatory language or image recognition. Entrepreneurs can play a crucial role in ensuring the ethical use of AI by training their AI systems on diverse, representative datasets, thereby mitigating bias.

Alongside bias, entrepreneurs must grapple with the ethical implications of using AI in fraud detection and cybersecurity. While AI can be a potent tool in detecting fraudulent activity and safeguarding sensitive data, it also raises concerns about privacy and surveillance. Entrepreneurs must strike a delicate balance, leveraging AI to enhance security measures while respecting the privacy rights of their customers and employees. By emphasizing this need for balance, we help entrepreneurs understand the ethical dilemma and the importance of a measured approach.

Another ethical consideration when implementing AI technologies is the potential impact on job displacement. As AI becomes more integrated across industries, there is growing concern about job losses due to automation. Entrepreneurs must be mindful of the social implications of AI adoption and consider ways to mitigate the adverse effects on employment.

Addressing ethical and bias concerns is vital for entrepreneurs and small businesses because it directly influences customer trust and reputation. Practical steps such as conducting regular bias audits, establishing ethical review committees, and staying up to date with AI ethics guidelines can help. By proactively tackling these issues through ongoing monitoring, companies can demonstrate their commitment to responsible AI use and foster stronger relationships with stakeholders.

Handling Resistance to AI Adoption

As an entrepreneur looking to implement artificial intelligence (AI) in your business, managing stakeholder resistance can be challenging. Addressing this head-on with clear strategies can help you feel capable and confident in leading your team through AI adoption.

First and foremost, it is essential to communicate the transformative benefits of AI adoption to all stakeholders. Whether it is the potential for increased efficiency, improved accuracy, or enhanced customer experience, clearly articulate how AI can revolutionize your business. Sharing success stories can inspire confidence and excitement about AI's positive impact.

Another vital strategy for handling resistance to AI adoption is involving all stakeholders in decision-making. By including employees, customers, and other critical stakeholders in the planning and implementation of AI technologies, you can help build a sense of shared purpose and confidence. This collaborative approach makes everyone feel valued and part of the journey toward innovation.

It is also crucial to provide adequate training and support for employees who will be using AI technologies. Many may feel intimidated or overwhelmed by the prospect of working with AI, so offering training programs and resources can help ease their concerns. Additionally, having a dedicated support team to address issues or questions can help ensure a smooth transition to AI adoption.

In some cases, resistance to AI adoption may stem from concerns about job security or the potential for job displacement. It is vital to address these concerns openly and honestly and to emphasize that AI technologies are meant to augment human capabilities, not replace them. By focusing on how AI can empower employees and enhance their work, you can help alleviate fears about job loss and instill a sense of security and confidence.

Finally, it is vital to continuously monitor and evaluate the impact of AI technologies on your business. Use key performance indicators (KPIs) such as customer satisfaction scores, operational efficiency metrics, and revenue growth to measure success. Collecting and analyzing this data helps demonstrate the tangible benefits of AI adoption and informs necessary adjustments. This ongoing evaluation process guides entrepreneurs in making data-driven decisions and building confidence in AI technologies.

Dealing with Technical Challenges and Limitations

In the world of artificial intelligence (AI), entrepreneurs and small businesses face many technical challenges and limitations when implementing AI. Recognizing issues like data quality and computing power can help you feel prepared and proactive in overcoming obstacles to unlock AI's full potential for your business.

One familiar technical challenge entrepreneurs and small businesses face is the quality and availability of data. AI models rely heavily on data to make accurate predictions and decisions, so having access to clean, relevant data is crucial. However, many businesses struggle to collect and organize data in a form usable for AI applications. This can lead to biased or inaccurate results, hindering the effectiveness of AI solutions. To address this challenge, businesses should invest in data quality tools and processes and explore external data sources to supplement their internal data.

Another technical limitation entrepreneurs and small businesses often encounter is computing power and budget constraints. AI models can be computationally intensive, requiring significant processing power and resources to run efficiently. For smaller businesses with limited budgets, this can pose a barrier to implementing AI solutions. To overcome this limitation, companies can consider cloud-based AI services that offer scalable computing power at a fraction of the cost of traditional on-premise solutions. Additionally, leveraging pre-trained AI models and open-source tools can help businesses achieve their AI goals without breaking the bank.

In the realm of AI applications such as natural language processing (NLP), computer vision and image recognition, fraud detection and cybersecurity, personalized marketing and recommendation systems, sentiment analysis and social media monitoring, robotics and automation, financial trading algorithms, and smart home technology and Internet of Things (IoT), entrepreneurs and small businesses may face unique technical challenges specific to each niche. For example, businesses implementing NLP may struggle with understanding nuances in language and context, while those working with computer vision may encounter issues with image quality and recognition accuracy. By understanding the specific challenges and limitations within their chosen AI niche, businesses can develop targeted strategies to address them effectively.

In conclusion, navigating the technical challenges and limitations of implementing AI in your business requires a strategic approach and a willingness to adapt to changing circumstances. By investing in data quality, exploring cost-effective computing solutions, and understanding the unique challenges of your chosen AI niche, entrepreneurs and small businesses can overcome obstacles and harness the power of AI to drive innovation and growth. With the right mindset and resources, the possibilities of AI are limitless for businesses of all sizes.

NINE

CASE STUDIES AND SUCCESS STORIES

Real-World Examples of AI Implementation in Small Businesses

In today's dynamic business environment, small businesses are increasingly adopting artificial intelligence (AI) to gain a competitive edge. AI, with its potential to streamline operations and enhance customer experiences, offers a transformative opportunity for small businesses. This subchapter will delve into real-world instances of AI implementation in small businesses across diverse industries, highlighting the tangible benefits they have reaped. This aims to inspire confidence and optimism about AI's possibilities.

One example of AI implementation in small businesses is the use of personalized marketing and recommendation systems. Companies can analyze customer data by leveraging AI algorithms to deliver personalized recommendations and targeted marketing campaigns. For instance, an e-commerce retailer can use AI to recommend products based on a customer's browsing history and purchase behavior, thereby increasing conversion rates and customer satisfaction.

Another everyday use case of AI in small businesses is fraud detection and cybersecurity. AI-powered fraud detection systems can analyze vast amounts of data in real time to identify suspicious activity and prevent fraudulent transactions. This is especially crucial for small businesses that may not have the resources to monitor and detect fraudulent activities manually.

In the realm of robotics and automation, AI is revolutionizing the way small businesses operate. From automating repetitive tasks to enhancing productivity, AI-powered robots are increasingly used across industries such as manufacturing, logistics, and healthcare. For example, a small manufacturing company can use AI-powered robots to automate its assembly line, increasing efficiency and reducing costs.

AI is also utilized in the financial industry, particularly in developing trading algorithms. Small businesses in the financial sector can leverage AI algorithms to analyze market trends, predict stock price movements, and execute trades at lightning speed. This can help small businesses stay ahead of the competition and maximize their investment returns.

Overall, the examples highlighted in this subchapter demonstrate the vast potential of AI to transform small businesses across industries. By embracing AI technologies such as natural language processing, computer vision, and sentiment analysis, small businesses can unlock new opportunities for growth, innovation, and success in today's digital economy. This should inspire hope and optimism in entrepreneurs and small businesses, showing them that the future is bright with AI.

Lessons Learned and Best Practices

In the fast-paced world of entrepreneurship, integrating artificial intelligence (AI) into your business can be a game-changer. However, it's essential to be aware of everyday challenges, such as limited resources, data quality issues, and gaps in technical expertise. Navigating these complexities, including data quality, scalability, and stakeholder alignment, can be daunting. This subchapter, "Lessons Learned and Best Practices," aims to equip entrepreneurs and small businesses with valuable insights and strategies to successfully overcome these challenges and integrate AI technologies into their operations.

One key lesson from successful AI adopters is that starting small and scaling gradually can boost your confidence. Identifying specific use cases where AI adds value and evaluating solutions within your budget helps you feel capable and motivated to begin your AI journey.

Focusing on data quality and preparation can give entrepreneurs a sense of control. Prioritizing data cleansing, normalization, and validation ensures your AI models are reliable, helping you feel more secure about your AI initiatives and fostering responsible use.

Involving key stakeholders from different departments can help entrepreneurs feel supported and engaged. Building a cross-functional team with AI, data science, and business expertise encourages collaboration and makes you feel part of a collective effort toward successful AI adoption.

Finally, in the ever-evolving field of AI, continuous learning and adaptation are not just beneficial but critical for staying ahead. Entrepreneurs should foster a culture of experimentation and innovation within their organizations to test new AI technologies and methodologies. By staying informed about the latest trends and advancements in AI, businesses can leverage cutting-edge solutions to drive growth, improve efficiency, and enhance customer experiences. Ultimately, embracing AI technologies can empower entrepreneurs and small businesses to unlock new opportunities and achieve sustainable success in today's digital economy.

Inspiration for Readers' Own AI Journey

Are you ready to embark on your AI journey? Whether you are an entrepreneur looking to implement artificial intelligence in your business or a small business owner interested in leveraging the power of AI, endless opportunities await you. In this subchapter, we will explore some key sources of inspiration to help you kickstart your AI journey and set yourself up for success in the rapidly evolving world of AI technology.

One of AI's most inspiring aspects is its ability to revolutionize industries and transform businesses' operations. From natural language processing

(NLP) to computer vision and image recognition, AI has the potential to enhance productivity, streamline processes, and drive innovation in a wide range of applications. By exploring the latest advancements in AI technology, entrepreneurs and small businesses can gain valuable insights into how to implement AI to solve real-world problems and create new growth opportunities.

Fraud detection and cybersecurity are critical areas where AI can significantly impact businesses. AI can help companies to protect their data and safeguard against cyber threats by leveraging AI algorithms and machine learning techniques. By leveraging AI algorithms and machine learning, companies can detect and prevent fraudulent activity in real time, ensuring the security and integrity of their operations. This aspect of AI provides a competitive advantage and inspires entrepreneurs to explore new possibilities in cybersecurity.

Personalized marketing and recommendation systems are another exciting area where AI can drive business success. By analyzing customer data and behavior patterns, AI algorithms can deliver personalized recommendations and targeted marketing campaigns that resonate with individual preferences and interests. This level of personalization enhances the customer experience and inspires entrepreneurs to think creatively about how AI can optimize marketing strategies and drive customer engagement.

Sentiment analysis and social media monitoring are essential tools for businesses looking to understand and respond to customer feedback and trends. By analyzing social media data and online conversations, AI can provide valuable insights into consumer sentiment, enabling businesses to make informed decisions and adapt their strategies accordingly. This aspect of AI is inspiring and empowers entrepreneurs to harness data analytics to gain a competitive edge in today's digital landscape.

In conclusion, the possibilities for entrepreneurs and small businesses to leverage AI technology are endless. Whether you are interested in robotics and automation, financial trading algorithms, smart home technology, or the Internet of Things (IoT), there is no shortage of inspiration to fuel your AI journey. By exploring the latest trends and advancements in AI technology, entrepreneurs can unlock new opportunities for growth, innovation, and success in the dynamic world of artificial intelligence. So, are you ready to take the next step on your AI journey? The future awaits.

TEN

LOOKING AHEAD

FUTURE TRENDS IN AI FOR SMALL BUSINESS

As artificial intelligence (AI) rapidly evolves, small businesses have a unique opportunity to enhance operations, improve customer experiences, and drive innovation. To capitalize on this, entrepreneurs should identify specific AI tools and strategies, such as chatbots or data analytics, that align with their goals. By staying ahead of emerging technologies and trends, entrepreneurs can remain competitive in today's dynamic market. In this chapter, we will delve into the future trends in AI for small businesses, exploring the broad opportunities and specific technologies poised to reshape the business landscape.

Emerging Technologies and Trends

The world of AI is a dynamic and ever-evolving landscape, offering small businesses a plethora of opportunities for growth and innovation. From personalized marketing campaigns that speak directly to your customers' needs to robust fraud detection systems that safeguard your business, the potential applications of AI can inspire entrepreneurs to see new paths for expansion and success.

Personalized Marketing and Recommendation Systems: One of the most promising trends in AI for small businesses is the rise of customized marketing and recommendation systems. By leveraging AI algorithms to analyze customer data and behavior, companies can deliver hyper-targeted content and product recommendations that resonate with individual preferences and needs. This level of personalization can make small business owners feel optimistic about building stronger, more meaningful customer relationships, increasing conversion rates, and fostering brand loyalty.

Fraud Detection and Cybersecurity: With cyber threats becoming increasingly sophisticated, businesses are turning to AI-powered solutions to protect their sensitive data and assets. Advanced fraud detection algorithms can proactively identify and mitigate potential risks, safeguarding operations and reputation in an increasingly digital world.

Robotics and Automation: AI-powered robotics and automation are not just buzzwords; they are revolutionizing business operations across industries. Imagine a manufacturing process that is not only efficient but also adaptable, or a customer service system that can handle multiple inquiries simultaneously. These are just a few examples of how AI can streamline processes, improve efficiency, and reduce costs. Small businesses can capitalize on this trend by integrating robotics and automation into their operations to gain a competitive edge.

Natural Language Processing (NLP) and Chatbots: NLP enables computers to understand and interpret human language, allowing businesses to automate tasks such as customer service inquiries, data entry, and content creation. By leveraging chatbots and other NLP-driven solutions, small businesses can save time and resources while delivering a more personalized, efficient customer experience.

Opportunities for Further Innovation and Growth

Small businesses, far from being left behind, have a wealth of opportunities to pioneer new innovations and drive growth with AI. However, concerns about costs, complexity, and data privacy may arise. By strategically embracing AI and addressing these challenges, entrepreneurs can unlock new levels of efficiency, productivity, and competitiveness, propelling their businesses into a future of endless possibilities.

Data-Driven Decision Making: AI enables small businesses to make informed decisions based on data-driven insights. Machine learning algorithms can accurately predict future trends, customer behavior, and market conditions by analyzing vast amounts of data. This insight empowers entrepreneurs to optimize their marketing strategies, streamline operations, and stay ahead of the competition.

Customer Engagement and Loyalty: Personalized marketing and recommendation systems enable businesses to connect with customers, fostering brand loyalty and boosting customer retention. Small companies can enhance the customer experience and build lasting relationships with their audience by delivering targeted content and product recommendations.

Efficiency and Productivity: Robotics and automation technologies streamline processes, reduce manual labor, and increase efficiency within small businesses. By automating repetitive tasks such as data entry, invoice processing, and inventory management, AI-driven solutions free up employees to focus on more strategic and creative tasks, driving productivity and innovation.

Preparing Your Business for Future Advancements

Small businesses, with their agility and adaptability, are well-positioned to harness the full potential of AI and thrive in today's fast-paced business environment. To begin, entrepreneurs can explore affordable AI tools, attend relevant training, or consult with AI specialists. By investing in talent, developing clear strategies, and prioritizing data quality and governance, entrepreneurs can confidently steer their businesses toward success in the digital age.

Investing in Talent: Hiring data scientists, AI engineers, and experts across various AI fields can help small businesses leverage AI to streamline operations and drive innovation. Additionally, investing in AI training programs for existing employees fosters a culture of continuous learning and innovation within the organization.

Developing Clear Strategies: Small businesses should develop clear AI strategies that align with their business goals and objectives. By identifying areas where AI can be most impactful and setting clear objectives for implementation, companies can ensure that their AI investments drive tangible results and support long-term growth.

Prioritizing Data Quality and Governance: Data quality and governance are essential for ensuring that AI algorithms and deployed models are accurate, reliable, and ethical. Small businesses should implement robust data collection and management processes, ensure data privacy and security, and establish guidelines for responsible AI use to build customer trust and comply with regulatory requirements.

Conclusion

As AI continues to reshape industries and redefine business operations, small businesses that strategically embrace these technologies gain a significant competitive advantage. By staying ahead of emerging trends, leveraging AI technologies effectively, and preparing for future advancements, entrepreneurs can drive innovation, improve efficiency, and achieve sustainable growth in the rapidly evolving digital landscape. The power of artificial intelligence is within your reach, and by embracing it, you can propel your small business into the future with confidence.

ELEVEN

ETHICAL CONSIDERATIONS AND RESPONSIBLE AI PRACTICES

Ensuring Fairness, Transparency, and Accountability

In the fast-paced world of Artificial Intelligence (AI), entrepreneurs and small businesses play a crucial role in ensuring fairness, transparency, and accountability in their AI implementations. This subchapter will empower you with the knowledge of these principles and provide practical tips for incorporating them into your business practices, making you a responsible and ethical AI adopter.

Fairness is essential for ethical AI practices because biased algorithms can cause discriminatory outcomes. Entrepreneurs and small businesses must evaluate their training data to ensure it reflects diverse populations and regularly monitor AI systems for bias, making adjustments to promote fairness and equity.

Transparency is another essential component of responsible AI implementation, and it's not as daunting as it may seem. Entrepreneurs and small businesses should strive to make their AI systems understandable and explainable to end users. Clarifying decision processes and being open about limitations can help the audience feel confident and reassured in their capacity to build trust and mitigate risks.

Accountability is crucial for ensuring that AI systems are used responsibly and ethically. Entrepreneurs and small businesses should establish clear lines of responsibility for AI decision-making, fostering a sense of pride and integrity in their commitment to ethical AI practices. Implementing oversight structures demonstrates their dedication to trustworthy operations.

In conclusion, ensuring fairness, transparency, and accountability in AI implementations is crucial for entrepreneurs and small businesses in today's digital landscape. By prioritizing these principles, companies can mitigate the risks of bias and discrimination and build trust with customers and stakeholders. By incorporating fairness, transparency, and accountability into their AI strategies, entrepreneurs and small businesses can unlock the full potential of AI technology while minimizing the potential for harm and maximizing the benefits for society.

Guidelines for Ethical AI Adoption

In today's rapidly evolving technological landscape, adopting artificial intelligence (AI) has become increasingly prevalent among entrepreneurs and small businesses seeking a competitive edge. However, great power comes with great responsibility, and companies must adhere to ethical guidelines when implementing AI. This subchapter provides a comprehensive overview of the fundamental principles and considerations entrepreneurs and small businesses should consider when adopting AI technology.

First and foremost, businesses must prioritize transparency and accountability in their AI adoption processes. This means being open and honest about how AI systems are used within the organization and ensuring mechanisms are in place to hold decision-makers accountable for the outcomes of AI-generated recommendations and actions. By fostering a culture of transparency and accountability, businesses can build trust with their customers and stakeholders while mitigating the risks of bias and discrimination arising from unchecked AI algorithms.

Secondly, businesses should prioritize fairness and equity in their AI adoption strategies. This means actively working to identify and mitigate bias in AI algorithms and ensuring that the benefits of AI technology are distributed equitably among all stakeholders. By taking proactive steps to address issues of fairness and equity, businesses can avoid potential backlash from customers, regulators, and the general public while maximizing the positive impact of AI technology on their operations.

Additionally, businesses should prioritize data privacy and security when adopting AI technology. This means implementing robust data protection measures, such as encryption and access controls, to safeguard sensitive information from unauthorized access or misuse. Businesses can build trust with their customers and stakeholders by prioritizing data privacy and security while complying with relevant data protection laws and regulations.

Furthermore, businesses should prioritize human oversight and control in their AI adoption processes. This means ensuring that humans are ultimately responsible for making critical decisions based on AI-generated insights, and that mechanisms are in place to intervene in the event of errors or malfunctions in AI systems. By maintaining human oversight and control, businesses can avoid potential ethical pitfalls and ensure AI technology is used responsibly in their operations.

In conclusion, the adoption of AI technology offers entrepreneurs and small businesses a unique opportunity to drive innovation and growth. However, with this opportunity comes the responsibility to adhere to ethical guidelines when implementing AI. By prioritizing transparency, fairness, data privacy, and human oversight in their AI adoption processes, businesses cannot only maximize the benefits of AI technology but also play a significant role in shaping the ethical landscape of AI.

Building Trust with Customers and Stakeholders

Building trust with customers and stakeholders is crucial for the success of any business, especially in the fast-paced world of artificial intelligence (AI). As entrepreneurs and small businesses navigate the complex landscape of AI technologies such as machine learning, natural language processing, computer vision, and fraud detection, it is essential to prioritize building solid relationships with those who interact with your products and services. Establishing trust can foster loyalty, drive growth, and differentiate your brand in a competitive market.

One way to build trust with customers and stakeholders is to be transparent about how AI is used in your business. Many people are wary of AI technologies and may have concerns about privacy, security, and ethical implications. By openly communicating about the algorithms and data sources used in your AI systems, you can demonstrate your commitment to integrity and accountability. This transparency can help alleviate fears and build confidence in your brand.

In addition to transparency, it is vital to prioritize data security and privacy when implementing AI in your business. Customers and stakeholders must know that their personal information is handled responsibly and ethically. By investing in robust cybersecurity measures and compliance with data protection regulations, you can show that you take the protection of sensitive data seriously. Building a trustworthy reputation in this area can help attract and retain customers who value privacy.

Another critical aspect of building trust with customers and stakeholders is delivering on your promises. Whether using AI for personalized marketing, sentiment analysis, or financial trading algorithms, it is crucial to ensure that your systems are reliable, accurate, and effective. You can build a reputation for excellence and reliability by consistently providing value and meeting expectations. This reliability can help you earn your customers' and stakeholders' trust, leading to long-term relationships and sustainable growth.

In conclusion, building trust with customers and stakeholders is essential for the success of your AI-driven business. By being transparent, prioritizing data security and privacy, and delivering on your promises, you can establish a strong foundation of trust that will set you apart in the competitive AI market. As entrepreneurs and small businesses in the AI industry, it is essential to prioritize building relationships based on trust and integrity to drive long-term success and growth.

TWELVE

PRACTICAL APPLICATIONS ACROSS INDUSTRIES

AI Applications in Marketing, Customer Service, Finance, Operations, etc.

AI technology has rapidly developed in recent years, offering practical applications for entrepreneurs and small businesses across multiple industries. One key area where AI is making a significant impact is marketing. Companies can use machine learning algorithms to analyze customer data to create personalized marketing campaigns targeting specific demographics. This improves customer engagement, increases conversion rates, and ultimately boosts sales.

In addition to marketing, AI is also revolutionizing customer service. Natural language processing (NLP) allows businesses to automate customer interactions through chatbots and virtual assistants, responding instantly to customer queries and concerns. For example, small retailers can implement chatbots to handle common questions, thereby enhancing customer satisfaction and reducing the workload for customer service teams, allowing them to focus on more complex issues.

Finance is another sector where AI is proving invaluable. Using algorithms and predictive analytics, small financial advisory firms can optimize their operations, identify potential risks, and make informed investment decisions. AI-powered fraud detection systems also prevent fraudulent activities, safeguarding businesses from financial losses.

Operations is another area where AI is reshaping business operations. By leveraging robotics and automation, businesses can streamline production processes, reduce human error, and increase efficiency. This saves time and resources and improves overall productivity and competitiveness in the market.

AI technology holds immense potential to revolutionize how entrepreneurs and small businesses operate, helping them feel confident in their ability to innovate and stay competitive. From marketing and customer service to finance and operations, AI offers businesses a wide range of opportunities to adapt and succeed. By embracing AI technology, companies can drive growth, improve efficiency, and build resilience in the evolving business landscape.

Industry-Specific Case Studies and Success Stories

This subchapter will showcase industry-specific case studies and success stories that can inspire entrepreneurs and small businesses to see AI as a practical tool. These real-world examples demonstrate how AI can transform various niches, encouraging readers to envision their own potential for innovation and growth.

One industry that has seen significant advancements in AI is financial trading. Financial institutions can now make faster and more accurate trading decisions using machine learning algorithms. For example, hedge funds have successfully implemented AI to analyze market trends and execute trades more optimally, leading to higher profits and reduced risk.

AI has proven to be a game-changer in fraud detection and cybersecurity. Banks and other financial institutions use AI-powered algorithms to detect and prevent fraudulent activities in real time. By analyzing large volumes of data and identifying patterns, AI systems can flag suspicious transactions and help businesses mitigate potential risks.

Another exciting application of AI is in personalized marketing and recommendation systems. E-commerce platforms like Amazon and

Netflix use AI algorithms to analyze customer behavior and preferences, delivering tailored recommendations that drive sales and improve customer satisfaction. By leveraging AI, businesses can enhance their marketing strategies and create more engaging customer experiences.

In robotics and automation, AI technologies are transforming industries such as manufacturing and logistics. Companies are deploying AI-powered robots to streamline production processes, optimize supply chain operations, and improve efficiency. These innovations increase productivity, reduce labor costs, and enhance workplace safety.

Overall, the success stories highlighted in this subchapter demonstrate the immense potential of AI across various industries. Entrepreneurs and small businesses can leverage AI technologies to drive innovation, improve decision-making, and stay ahead of the competition. By studying these case studies, companies can gain valuable insights into effectively implementing AI in their operations and unlock new growth opportunities.

Tailoring AI Solutions to Different Business Sectors

Artificial intelligence (AI) has become indispensable for businesses across sectors, offering adaptable solutions that empower entrepreneurs and small businesses to meet their unique needs. In this subchapter, we will explore how customizing AI solutions can help businesses feel capable and confident in their ability to innovate and succeed within their industry's specific context.

One key consideration when implementing AI in different business sectors is understanding each industry's challenges and opportunities. For example, in artificial intelligence and machine learning, businesses may benefit from predictive analytics models that forecast market trends and customer behavior. On the other hand, natural language processing (NLP) can be leveraged in industries such as healthcare and legal services to analyze and interpret vast amounts of text data.

AI can streamline manufacturing and retail processes in computer vision and image recognition, allowing businesses to automate quality control and inventory management tasks. Fraud detection and cybersecurity are also critical areas where AI can be tailored to identify and prevent cyber threats in real-time, protecting sensitive data and maintaining customer trust.

Personalized marketing and recommendation systems are another area where AI can be customized to target specific audiences and deliver tailored content to individual customers. Sentiment analysis and social media monitoring are valuable tools for businesses to gauge public opinion and sentiment toward their brand. At the same time, robotics and automation can streamline operations in logistics and manufacturing.

Financial trading algorithms, smart home technology, and Internet of Things (IoT) devices are additional sectors where AI solutions can be tailored to optimize performance and drive innovation. By understanding each business sector's unique needs and challenges, entrepreneurs and small businesses can harness the power of AI to stay ahead of the competition and drive success in the digital age.

THIRTEEN

SCALING UP
DEPLOYING AI SOLUTIONS

Prototyping, Testing, and Iterative Development

In the subchapter "Prototyping, Testing, and Iterative Development," entrepreneurs and small businesses in the AI and machine learning niche will learn how prototyping and testing can build their confidence and motivation by refining solutions to meet specific needs.

Prototyping involves creating a preliminary version of the AI solution to test its functionality and usability. For instance, a retail business might develop a prototype of an AI-powered chatbot to handle customer inquiries. This allows entrepreneurs to gather stakeholder feedback and make necessary adjustments before moving forward with full-scale development. By taking an iterative approach to prototyping, entrepreneurs can quickly identify and address any issues or limitations in the AI technology, ultimately saving time and resources in the long run.

Testing is another critical component of the development process. Entrepreneurs must rigorously test their AI solutions to ensure accuracy, reliability, and security. This involves running various scenarios and use cases, such as stress testing to see how the AI system handles high volumes of data, and security testing to identify any vulnerabilities. By conducting thorough testing, entrepreneurs can mitigate risks and improve the overall quality of their AI solutions.

Iterative development is an ongoing process involving continuously refining and enhancing AI technology based on feedback and insights from prototyping and testing. This approach not only allows entrepreneurs to adapt to changing requirements and market conditions but also opens the door to innovation and growth. By embracing iterative development, entrepreneurs can stay ahead of the curve and deliver cutting-edge AI solutions that drive business growth and innovation.

Overall, prototyping, testing, and iterative development are not just essential practices but empowering tools for entrepreneurs and small businesses looking to implement AI technology successfully. Emphasizing how these practices improve AI robustness and reliability will help readers understand their critical role in achieving market-ready solutions. By following these best practices, companies can develop robust and reliable AI solutions that meet the evolving needs of their customers and the market. With a focus on continuous improvement and innovation, entrepreneurs can leverage the power of AI to drive business success in various niches, from personalized marketing to financial trading algorithms.

Scaling AI Solutions for Production

Scaling AI solutions for production is a key step that can empower entrepreneurs and small businesses to feel optimistic about expanding their impact through effective strategies.

When scaling AI solutions for production, one key consideration is ensuring the infrastructure can support the increased workload. This may involve investing in more powerful hardware or cloud computing resources to handle the increased computational demands of running AI models in a production environment. However, this can be a significant financial investment. Entrepreneurs and small businesses should also consider implementing robust data pipelines and data management systems to ensure AI models have access to the data needed to make accurate predictions. This can be a complex process, requiring the integration of various data sources and the implementation of data governance policies.

Another essential aspect of scaling AI solutions for production is monitoring and maintenance. As AI models are deployed at scale, it is necessary to continuously monitor their performance and make adjustments to ensure optimal results. This may involve setting up alerts and automated monitoring systems to detect issues in real time and take corrective action promptly. Regular maintenance and updates are also necessary to keep AI models running smoothly and up to date with the latest data and techniques.

Collaboration and teamwork are essential when scaling AI solutions for production. Entrepreneurs and small businesses should involve cross-functional teams from different departments, including data scientists, engineers, and business analysts, to ensure AI solutions align with business goals and objectives. Effective communication and collaboration between team members are crucial for successfully scaling AI solutions for production and driving business outcomes.

In conclusion, scaling AI solutions for production requires careful planning, infrastructure investment, monitoring, maintenance, and collaboration among cross-functional teams. By following the strategies outlined in this subchapter, entrepreneurs and small businesses can effectively deploy AI solutions at scale and realize the benefits of artificial intelligence in their operations. With the right approach and mindset, AI can be a powerful tool for driving business growth and innovation in various industries and niches.

Managing Growth and Expansion with AI

Managing growth and expansion can be a thrilling but challenging journey for entrepreneurs and small businesses in today's fast-paced business environment. However, with the help of artificial intelligence (AI), this process can be transformed into an exciting adventure of discovery and innovation. This subchapter will take you on this adventure, exploring how AI can be leveraged to facilitate growth and expansion in various areas of your business. Highlighting how AI-driven insights inform strategic decisions will help readers see the tangible benefits of adopting AI for growth management.

One key benefit of using AI to manage growth and expansion is its ability to analyze large amounts of data quickly and accurately. However, this also poses a risk of data privacy and security breaches. With AI-powered analytics tools, entrepreneurs can gain valuable insights into customer behavior, market trends, and competitive landscapes. This information can then be used to make informed decisions about expanding into new markets, launching new products or services, or scaling existing operations. However, it's essential to ensure that the data used for analysis is anonymized and secure to protect customer privacy and business interests.

Another way AI can help entrepreneurs manage growth and expansion is through automation. By implementing AI-powered systems and processes, businesses can streamline operations, reduce manual workloads, and increase productivity. For example, AI-powered chatbots can handle customer inquiries and support, freeing up valuable time for employees to focus on other strategic tasks. This not only improves operational efficiency but also enhances the customer experience, thereby increasing customer satisfaction and loyalty.

AI can also play a crucial role in fraud detection and cybersecurity, which are essential considerations for businesses looking to expand their online presence. However, there are ethical implications to consider, such as the potential for AI to be biased or discriminatory. Companies can use AI algorithms to monitor and analyze user behavior to detect suspicious activities and prevent security breaches. This protects the business and its customers and builds trust and credibility in the marketplace. However, it's essential to ensure that the AI algorithms are trained on unbiased data and are regularly audited to detect and correct any biases.

Furthermore, AI can enhance personalized marketing and recommendation systems, helping businesses target customers with the right products or services at the right time. By analyzing customer data and preferences, AI algorithms can deliver personalized recommendations, promotions, and offers that drive engagement and loyalty. This level of personalization can significantly improve customer satisfaction and retention rates, ultimately driving sustainable growth and expansion.

Entrepreneurs and small businesses can effectively manage growth and expansion in a competitive, dynamic market by harnessing AI's capabilities in natural language processing, computer vision, sentiment analysis, and robotics. These may sound like complex terms, but in simple terms, they refer to AI's ability to understand and interpret human language, recognize and interpret images and videos, analyze and understand human emotions, and interact with the physical world. Businesses in the AI niche must embrace these technologies and leverage their capabilities to stay ahead of the curve and drive continued success in the digital age.

CONCLUSION

Embracing the Future of AI in Small Business

As we conclude our exploration into the transformative potential of artificial intelligence (AI) for small businesses, we must reflect on the key insights and takeaways that highlight how AI can drive growth and innovation. Throughout this journey, we've delved into practical applications, challenges, and opportunities AI offers in today's rapidly evolving business landscape. Let's recap some of the crucial points covered and consider how small business owners, regardless of their technical background, can harness AI to improve operations and stay competitive.

Practical Applications of AI

Our journey began by exploring real-world examples of AI in small business operations. For instance, a small e-commerce business used natural language processing (NLP) to automate customer service responses, reducing response times and boosting customer satisfaction. A local restaurant implemented computer vision to monitor food quality, maintain standards, and reduce waste. These examples show how AI, which simulates human intelligence in machines, can streamline processes, enhance efficiency, and improve customer experiences. Leveraging AI solutions enables small businesses to automate tasks, extract insights from data, and make smarter decisions for growth.

Mindset Shift and Continuous Learning

A crucial aspect of integrating AI into small business operations is fostering a mindset shift and committing to continuous learning. While AI offers immense benefits, it also comes with its share of challenges. These can include the initial cost of implementation, which may involve purchasing new hardware or software, the need for skilled personnel who understand AI technologies, and the potential for data breaches, which can be mitigated by investing in cybersecurity measures. However, by embracing AI technologies and staying informed about the latest trends and developments, small business owners can position themselves at the forefront of innovation and gain a competitive edge in their industries. Investing in talent and resources, attending workshops and conferences, and seeking encouragement from peers and mentors are essential steps in this transformation journey.

Data Security and Privacy

Our discussion also emphasized the importance of prioritizing data security and privacy when implementing AI in small businesses. As AI relies heavily on data collection and analysis, ensuring compliance with relevant regulations and standards, such as the General Data Protection Regulation (GDPR), is imperative. Small businesses can mitigate risks and liabilities associated with AI deployment by prioritizing data protection and building customer trust. This can be achieved by establishing robust data governance processes that set policies and procedures for data management, and by investing in cybersecurity measures, such as encryption and secure data storage, which are critical components of a successful AI strategy.

Opportunities for Growth and Innovation

Looking ahead, the opportunities for growth and innovation presented by AI are vast and varied for small businesses. Whether automating routine tasks, such as data entry or inventory management, personalizing customer interactions through chatbots or recommendation systems, or predicting market trends to inform business strategies, AI offers endless possibilities for driving efficiency, productivity, and profitability. By aligning AI initiatives with business goals and objectives, small business owners can unlock new opportunities for expansion and differentiation in today's digital economy. This can help you feel more confident about leveraging AI for your business growth.

Final Thoughts

In conclusion, the transformative power of AI for small businesses is not just a possibility; it's a beacon of hope and optimism. By adopting AI technologies, entrepreneurs can revolutionize their operations, delight customers, and stay ahead of the competition. However, success in the AI-driven future requires more than technological adoption;it demands a strategic approach, a commitment to learning, and a focus on ethical and responsible AI deployment. As we continue on this journey of innovation, let us harness the full potential of AI to create a brighter, more prosperous future for small businesses everywhere, filled with hope and optimism. You can feel inspired to embrace AI as a tool for positive change.

We value your feedback and believe it's crucial for our continuous improvement! If you found this exploration of AI in small businesses informative and beneficial, we would greatly appreciate it if you could spare a moment to share your thoughts with a review. Your feedback can offer valuable insights to others considering the transformative power of AI in their businesses. Thank you for joining us on this journey, and may your endeavors in the realm of AI be met with success and prosperity. Remember, you're not alone in this journey. Community support can help you feel more encouraged and connected.

Conclusion

https://qr.link/AdwytZ

APPENDIX
COMPREHENSIVE GLOSSARY OF AI TERMS

Artificial Intelligence (AI): The simulation of human intelligence processes by machines, especially computer systems, to perform tasks that typically require human intelligence, such as visual perception, speech recognition, decision-making, and language translation. This technology is used in various fields, from healthcare to finance, to enhance efficiency and accuracy. Recognizing these applications can inspire your interest in AI's potential to transform industries.

Machine Learning (ML): A subset of AI that enables systems to learn and improve from experience without being explicitly programmed. Machine learning algorithms allow computers to identify patterns in data and make predictions or decisions based on them. For instance, ML is used in email spam filters to learn from the user's actions and improve its filtering accuracy over time.

Deep Learning: A specialized form of machine learning that uses neural networks with many layers (deep neural networks) to learn from large amounts of data. Neural networks are the foundational models that deep learning builds upon, consisting of interconnected nodes that mimic brain activity, helping readers understand their relationship.

Reinforcement Learning: Reinforcement learning is a type of machine learning that uses rewards and punishments to teach computers how to

Appendix

make decisions. By incentivizing desirable behaviors, reinforcement learning algorithms can learn to optimize processes and solve complex problems in real-world environments.

Neural Network: A computational model inspired by the structure and function of the human brain's neural networks. Neural networks consist of interconnected nodes (neurons) organized in layers, each processing input data and passing it to the next layer for further processing.

Natural Language Processing (NLP): A branch of AI that enables computers to understand, interpret, and generate human language. NLP algorithms analyze and process text and speech data to extract meaning, perform sentiment analysis, and facilitate language translation.

Computer Vision: A field of AI that enables computers to interpret and understand visual information from images or videos. Computer vision algorithms can recognize objects, detect patterns, and extract meaningful insights from visual data.

Speech Recognition: The ability of a computer system to recognize and transcribe spoken language into text. It enables hands-free interaction with devices, voice-controlled assistants, and automated transcription of spoken content.

Sentiment Analysis: Involves analyzing text data to determine the emotional tone expressed in it. Sentiment analysis algorithms classify text as positive, negative, or neutral, enabling businesses to understand customer opinions and reactions.

Predictive Analytics: Using statistical techniques and machine learning algorithms to analyze historical data and predict future events or trends. Predictive analytics helps businesses identify patterns, forecast outcomes, and optimize decision-making processes.

Robotics: The interdisciplinary field of engineering and science that involves the design, construction, operation, and use of robots. Robots are programmable machines capable of performing tasks autonomously or under human supervision, often incorporating AI technologies for perception, navigation, and decision-making.

Appendix

Automation: Using technology to perform tasks or processes with minimal human intervention. Automation systems can streamline operations, reduce errors, and increase efficiency by automating repetitive or labor-intensive tasks.

Fraud Detection: Identifying and preventing fraudulent activities or transactions using AI-powered algorithms and techniques. Fraud detection systems analyze patterns, anomalies, and suspicious behavior to detect and mitigate potential fraud risks.

Personalized Marketing: Delivering targeted marketing content or product recommendations tailored to individual preferences, behaviors, and demographics. Customized marketing strategies leverage AI algorithms to analyze customer data and deliver relevant, timely messages to enhance customer engagement and drive conversions.

Internet of Things (IoT): A network of interconnected devices embedded with sensors, software, and other technologies that enable them to collect and exchange data over the internet. IoT devices span a range of domains, including smart home appliances, wearable devices, industrial machinery, and environmental sensors.

Data Science: An interdisciplinary field that involves extracting insights and knowledge from structured and unstructured data using scientific methods, algorithms, and techniques. Data scientists analyze data, build predictive models, and derive actionable insights to inform decision-making processes.

Augmented Reality (AR): A technology that overlays digital information or virtual objects onto the real-world environment, typically viewed through a smartphone, tablet, or wearable device. AR applications enhance users' perception of reality by seamlessly blending virtual and physical elements.

Virtual Reality (VR): A technology that immerses users in a computer-generated virtual environment, typically experienced through a head-mounted display or VR headset. VR enables users to fully immerse themselves in virtual worlds, simulations, and experiences.

Blockchain: A decentralized, distributed ledger technology that records transactions across multiple computers in a tamper-resistant and

Appendix

transparent manner. Blockchain technology ensures data integrity, security, and trust in peer-to-peer transactions, with applications ranging from cryptocurrency to supply chain management.

Chatbot: A computer program or AI-powered system that simulates a conversation with human users through text or speech interfaces. Chatbots use natural language processing algorithms to understand user queries and provide relevant real-time responses or assistance.

This glossary provides a comprehensive overview of key terms and concepts in artificial intelligence (AI). As AI continues to evolve and shape industries across healthcare and finance, understanding these terms is not just informative but also essential for staying ahead in the AI revolution. Mastering these concepts can open new opportunities and boost your professional development.

APPENDIX
CHECKLIST FOR AI READINESS ASSESSMENT

1. **Define Business Objectives:** Clearly outline your business objectives and goals for integrating AI technologies. Highlight how AI can support strategic priorities to inspire confidence in its potential value.
2. **Assess Data Availability and Quality:** Evaluate the availability and quality of your data sources. Ensuring data accuracy and completeness will build trust in AI results and encourage commitment to data efforts.
3. **Evaluate IT Infrastructure:** Review your existing IT infrastructure and assess its compatibility with AI technologies. Ensure your infrastructure can support AI applications' computational and storage requirements and consider potential upgrades or investments if necessary.
4. **Identify Skill Gaps:** Identify AI-related skill gaps within your organization. Determine if you have the necessary expertise in data science, machine learning, and AI development, and consider training or hiring initiatives to fill any gaps.
5. **Assess Regulatory Compliance:** Evaluate regulatory requirements and compliance considerations related to AI deployment in your industry. Ensure your AI initiatives comply

with relevant data privacy, security, and ethical standards, such as GDPR or HIPAA.
6. **Review Budget and Resources:** Allocate resources for AI initiatives, including investment in technology infrastructure, talent acquisition, and ongoing maintenance and support. Determine the financial feasibility of AI projects and prioritize initiatives based on available resources.
7. **Conduct Stakeholder Analysis:** Identify key stakeholders and decision-makers within your organization who will be involved in AI initiatives. Engaging stakeholders effectively will foster a sense of inclusion and shared purpose in AI adoption.
8. **Evaluate Vendor Solutions:** Research and evaluate AI vendors and solutions that align with your business needs and objectives. Consider factors such as functionality, scalability, ease of integration, and vendor reputation, like industry experience and customer reviews, to select solutions that best support your AI strategy and ensure long-term success.
9. **Develop AI Strategy and Roadmap:** Develop a comprehensive AI strategy and roadmap that outlines the steps for implementing AI initiatives within your organization. Define project timelines, milestones, and success metrics-such as accuracy, efficiency gains, or ROI-to measure the impact of AI deployment and ensure alignment with business goals.
10. **Establish Governance and Risk Management:** Establish governance frameworks and risk management protocols to oversee AI initiatives and mitigate potential risks. Define roles and responsibilities, establish data governance policies, and monitor AI performance and compliance regularly.
11. **Pilot AI Projects:** Start with pilot projects to test the feasibility and effectiveness of AI technologies within your organization. Select small-scale projects with clear objectives and measurable outcomes to validate AI capabilities and demonstrate value to stakeholders.
12. **Monitor and Iterate:** Continuously monitor AI performance and iterate on AI models and algorithms based on feedback and insights gathered during deployment. Implement continuous

improvement processes to optimize AI performance and drive ongoing innovation.

By following this checklist, organizations can assess their readiness for AI adoption and lay the foundation for successfully implementing and integrating AI technologies into their business operations.

APPENDIX

SAMPLE AI IMPLEMENTATION ROADMAP

Assessment and Planning Phase

- Define Business Objectives: Clarify Business Objectives by pinpointing specific goals AI should support, such as operational efficiency or revenue growth, to guide strategic planning
- Conduct AI Readiness Assessment: Leave no stone unturned in evaluating the organization's readiness for AI implementation. Assess data availability, IT infrastructure, skill gaps, regulatory compliance, budget, and resources to ensure a solid foundation for your AI journey.
- Stakeholder Engagement: Your role is crucial. Engaging key stakeholders and decision-makers fosters a sense of shared purpose and commitment, which is vital for the success of AI initiatives.

Research and Vendor Selection

- Research AI Solutions: Explore available AI technologies and vendors that align with the organization's needs and objectives. Consider factors such as functionality, scalability, ease of integration, and cost.

Appendix

- Evaluate Vendor Solutions: Conduct demos and trials of shortlisted AI solutions to assess their capabilities and suitability for the organization's requirements.
- Select AI Vendors: Choose AI vendors based on thorough evaluation and selection criteria, such as their track record, customer reviews, and pricing. Negotiate contracts and agreements as needed, ensuring the vendor's services align with your business needs and objectives.

Data Preparation and Infrastructure Setup

- Data Assessment and Cleanup: Evaluate existing data sources, perform cleaning, and ensure data privacy to improve AI model accuracy and maintain security standards
- Infrastructure Evaluation: Assess the organization's IT infrastructure and determine if upgrades or enhancements are needed to support AI implementation. Consider factors such as computational power, storage capacity, and network capabilities.

Talent Acquisition and Training

- Identify Skill Gaps: Determine if the organization has the necessary expertise in data science, machine learning, and AI development. Identify skill gaps and plan for talent acquisition or training initiatives as needed.
- Employee Training: Provide training programs and resources to upskill existing employees on AI concepts, tools, and technologies relevant to their roles and responsibilities.

Pilot Project Development

- Define Pilot Project Objectives: Clearly articulate the pilot AI project's objectives, scope, and success criteria to help your team feel purposeful and confident in demonstrating AI's value.
- Data Modeling and Development: Develop AI models and algorithms aligned with the identified business objectives and the

available data for the pilot project. Test and refine the models to ensure accuracy and effectiveness.

Deployment and Integration

- Pilot Project Deployment: Deploy the developed AI solution in a controlled environment for testing and validation. Monitor the AI system's performance and functionality and gather user feedback.
- Integration with Existing Systems: Integrate the AI solution with existing business systems and processes to ensure seamless operation and data flow. This process involves collaborating with IT teams and stakeholders to address any integration challenges, ensuring that the AI solution is compatible with your existing systems and does not disrupt your business operations.

Evaluation and Optimization

- Performance Evaluation: Evaluate the deployed AI solution's performance against predefined success metrics and business objectives. Gather user and stakeholder feedback to identify areas for improvement.
- Continuous Improvement: Iterate the AI models and algorithms based on feedback and insights gathered during deployment. Implement optimizations and enhancements to improve AI performance, accuracy, and reliability.

Scaling and Expansion

- Scaling Pilot Projects: Once a pilot project has demonstrated its feasibility and value, it can be scaled to larger deployments across relevant business units or departments. This process involves identifying the necessary resources, addressing scalability issues, and ensuring the AI solution continues to meet business objectives as it scales up.
- Monitor and Manage Growth: Track the scalability and performance of AI solutions as they are rolled out across the

Appendix

organization. Implement strategies to manage growth effectively and ensure continued success.

Governance and Compliance

- Establish Governance Framework: Develop governance policies and procedures to oversee AI initiatives. This framework should include data governance, ethics, and compliance with regulatory requirements. Its role is to ensure that your AI initiatives are conducted ethically and in compliance, protecting your business and customers from potential risks.
- Risk Management: Identify and mitigate potential risks associated with AI implementation, including data security breaches, bias in AI algorithms, and regulatory non-compliance. Implement risk management protocols and controls to safeguard against risks.

Ongoing Support and Maintenance

- Provide Ongoing Support: Committing to continuous technical support and maintenance reassures your team that their efforts are valued and that AI solutions will be reliably sustained.
- Monitor Trends and Updates: Stay informed about emerging trends and best practices in AI. Continuously assess the organization's AI strategy and roadmap to adapt to changing market dynamics and technological advancements.

By following this AI implementation roadmap, small businesses can effectively plan, deploy, and manage AI initiatives to drive innovation, efficiency, and growth.

APPENDIX
RESOURCES FOR FURTHER LEARNING

In the ever-evolving landscape of artificial intelligence (AI), entrepreneurs and small business owners, regardless of their level of AI knowledge, can find accessible resources to support their learning and growth. This should help you feel supported and capable of engaging with AI, no matter your starting point. This subchapter will provide a curated list of resources tailored to entrepreneurs and small businesses looking to leverage AI for innovation and growth.

Here are some reputable resources for further learning on AI:

Online Courses

- Thrive Collective: Offers a variety of AI and Automation-related courses https://thrivecollectivehq.com/training-courses
- Coursera: Offers a variety of AI-related courses from top universities and institutions, including 'Machine Learning' by Stanford University and 'Deep Learning Specialization' by deeplearning.ai, which can be tailored to your industry needs for practical application.
- edX: Provides courses on AI and machine learning, such as "Artificial Intelligence (AI)" by Columbia University and "Introduction to Deep Learning" by Microsoft.

Appendix

- Udacity: Offers nano degree programs in AI, machine learning, and deep learning, designed to provide hands-on experience and practical skills.

Books

- Thrive Collective: Offers a variety of AI and Automation-related books https://thrivecollectivehq.com/books-and-journals
- "Artificial Intelligence: A Guide for Thinking Humans" by Melanie Mitchell: A comprehensive overview of AI concepts and their societal implications, accessible to non-technical readers.
- "Deep Learning" by Ian Goodfellow, Yoshua Bengio, and Aaron Courville: A definitive textbook on deep learning, covering theory, algorithms, and applications.
- "Hands-On Machine Learning with Scikit-Learn, Keras, and TensorFlow" by Aurélien Géron: A practical guide to machine learning and deep learning with Python libraries.

Online Platforms

- Kaggle: A platform for data science and machine learning competitions, as well as datasets, kernels (code notebooks), and tutorials.
- GitHub: Offers repositories with open-source AI projects, libraries, and resources for learning and collaboration.
- Towards Data Science: A publication on Medium featuring articles, tutorials, and case studies on data science, machine learning, and AI.

Podcasts

- "Machine Learning Guide" by OCDevel: A podcast series covering various topics in machine learning, AI research, and practical applications. New episodes are released every week, making it an excellent resource for staying up to date on the latest trends in AI.
- "The AI Podcast" by NVIDIA: Explores the latest advancements in

AI, featuring interviews with researchers, industry experts, and thought leaders.
- "Artificial Intelligence in Industry" by Emerj: Focuses on AI applications and trends in different industries, with insights from business leaders and experts.

YouTube Channels

- Two-Minute Papers: Provides short video summaries of recent AI research papers and breakthroughs in the field. These concise videos are perfect for busy entrepreneurs who want to stay up to date on the latest AI research in a short amount of time.
- Siraj Raval: This site offers tutorials, code walkthroughs, and discussions on AI, machine learning, and deep learning concepts.
- Sentdex: Covers tutorials and projects on AI, machine learning, natural language processing, and computer vision using Python libraries.

Professional Organizations and Conferences

- Association for the Advancement of Artificial Intelligence (AAAI): Provides resources, conferences, and publications on AI research and applications. Joining this organization can give you access to a network of AI professionals and the latest research in the field.
- NeurIPS (Conference on Neural Information Processing Systems): One of the premier conferences for AI and machine learning research, featuring presentations, workshops, and tutorials. The conference covers a wide range of topics, from the latest advancements in deep learning to the ethical implications of AI.

These resources offer a mix of theoretical knowledge, practical skills, and industry insights, all directly relevant to your business goals. Whether you're a beginner or an experienced practitioner, exploring these resources can help you stay informed and engaged in the rapidly evolving field of artificial intelligence and leverage its potential for your business.

A QUICK FAVOR

If you enjoyed this book, please consider leaving an honest review where you purchased it. Your feedback helps support the author and independent publishing, and even a sentence or two can make a big difference.

Thank you for reading and supporting independent publishing. Your support means a lot and helps authors continue creating.

ABOUT KIMBERLY BURK CORDOVA

Kimberly Burk Cordova is an author, entrepreneur, and the founder of **Thrive Collective**. This platform supports creators, leaders, and entrepreneurs through publishing, leadership development, and practical tools for real-life growth. With over **30 years of experience** in leadership, technology, and business transformation, she is recognized for transforming big ideas into actionable strategies that deliver results.

Kimberly writes across topics that reflect a life fueled by curiosity: travel and culture, business and leadership, technology and modern work, food and cooking, and the everyday lessons of family life. Her wide-ranging interests invite the audience to see her as relatable and engaging.

Now based in **Santa Fe, New Mexico**, Kimberly finds inspiration in the region's art, culture, and landscapes. She shares life with her husband, Greg, and is a proud mom and grandmother to Vera and Tillman, which adds a personal touch that fosters familiarity and trust.

Connect & Explore

- **Thrive Collective** (publishing, leadership, tools): https://www.ThriveCollectiveHQ.com
- **Code Prospector** (audiobook promo codes & reviews): https://www.TheCodeProspector.com
- **Wildflower Artisans** (small-batch silver + genuine stones, curated in Santa Fe): https://wildflowerartisans.com

- amazon.com/author/kimberlycordova
- goodreads.com/kbcordova
- youtube.com/@ThriveCollectiveHQ
- facebook.com/ThriveCollectiveHQ
- linkedin.com/in/kbcord
- tiktok.com/@ThriveCollectiveHQ
- instagram.com/thrivecollecthq
- pinterest.com/ThriveCollectiveHQ
- x.com/ThriveCoHQ

JOIN OUR MAILING LIST

Stay Connected with Thrive Collective

Love history, true crime, leadership insights, and travel guides? Stay in the loop with exclusive updates, behind-the-scenes content, and early access to upcoming releases from Thrive Collective. We value your interest and want you to feel part of our community.

📚 Be the first to hear about new books, special promotions, and subscriber-only content! Your early access makes you a key part of our journey.

✨ **Join now** and never miss a story, insight, or adventure. Stay connected with interests that matter to you and be part of something bigger.

https://thrivecollectivehq.com/contact

ALSO BY THRIVE COLLECTIVE

Shadows of the Past Series: by Eliza Hawthorne

- The Vanishing Heiress
- The Music of Murder
- The Silent Witness
- Whispers from the Murder Farm
- Architect of Desire
- The Vanishing Act (Trilogy Collection)

The Growth Leader Collection: by Kimberly Burk Cordova

- The Emotional Intelligence Advantage
- The Leadership Alchemist
- Turning Chaos into Gold
- Leadership Unlocked
- Lead Like You Mean It
- The Procrastination Cure
- Mind Games Exposed

AI & Automation Blueprint Series: by Kimberly Burk Cordova

- Digital Mastery Guide: AI for Productivity
- Digital Mastery Guide: AI Profit Masterclass
- Digital Mastery Guide: Google Ads AI Expertise
- Digital Mastery Guide: Automation in Small Businesses
- Digital Mastery Guide: Business Systemization
- Digital Mastery Guide: AI YouTube Masterclass
- Digital Mastery Guide: Necessary Online Business Tools
- Digital Mastery Guide: Metaverse Explained

The Profitable Seller Series: by Kimberly Burk Cordova

- FBA Freedom Formula
- Clicks That Convert
- Dropship Mastery

Profit & Protect: by Kimberly Burk Cordova

- Create It Once, Sell It Forever
- Launch & Leverage
- Udemy Income Mastery

Empowering Small Businesses Series: by Kimberly Burk Cordova

- The Entrepreneur's Edge
- Artificial Intelligence Unleashed
- Cybersecurity for Entrepreneurs
- Augmented and Virtual Reality

Campaigns That Convert: by Kimberly Burk Cordova

- The SEO Blueprint
- Affiliate Mastery Blueprint

Travel Series: by Kimberly Burk Cordova

- Santa Fe Uncovered
- Santa Fe
- Denver Dossier
- Portland Your Way
- Stress Relief Travel Coloring Book For Adults

Eat Without Fear Series: by Kimberly Burk Cordova

- Eat Light, Live Bright: Low-Fat Recipes & Meal Plans

Kitchen-Table Guide from a Tech Oma: by Kimberly Burk Cordova

- Kids + AI

Content Strategy Ladder: by Kimberly Burk Cordova

- Audience X-Ray Vision

Young Legends: Inspiring True Stories of Kids' Favorite Athletes, Leaders, and Inventors

- Basketball Legends for Kids
- Soccer Legends for Kids
- Game Changers: Women Athletes
- Baseball Legends You Should Know
- The Caveman's Guide to Mental Toughness for Young Athletes

Journal Series: by Cordova Creations

- Align & Shine
- The 369 Method Manifestation
- Disconnect To Reconnect
- Simplify Your Life
- Just Write
- I Am Too Old for This Sh*t
- Dear Mom and Dad
- My Cat Rocks
- My Dog Rocks
- My Soft Girl Rocks
- My Inner Badass Rocks
- My Son Rocks

- My Daughter Rocks
- My Husband Rocks
- My Wife Rocks

BIBLIOGRAPHY

Books and Reports

- Brynjolfsson, E., & McAfee, A. (2014). *The Second Machine Age: Work, Progress, and Prosperity in a Time of Brilliant Technologies*. W.W. Norton & Company.
- Russell, S., & Norvig, P. (2020). *Artificial Intelligence: A Modern Approach* (4th ed.). Pearson.
- Davenport, T. H., & Ronanki, R. (2018). *Artificial Intelligence for the Real World*. Harvard Business Review Press.
- Marr, B. (2018). *Artificial Intelligence in Practice: How 50 Successful Companies Used AI and Machine Learning to Solve Problems*. Wiley.
- Domingos, P. (2015). *The Master Algorithm: How the Quest for the Ultimate Learning Machine Will Remake Our World*. Basic Books.
- Goodfellow, I., Bengio, Y., & Courville, A. (2016). *Deep Learning*. MIT Press.
- Chollet, F. (2017). *Deep Learning with Python*. Manning Publications.
- Sutton, R. S., & Barto, A. G. (2018). *Reinforcement Learning: An Introduction*. MIT Press.
- Murphy, K. P. (2012). *Machine Learning: A Probabilistic Perspective*. MIT Press.
- Shalev-Shwartz, S., & Ben-David, S. (2014). *Understanding Machine Learning: From Theory to Algorithms*. Cambridge University Press.
- Jordan, M. I., & Mitchell, T. M. (2015). *Machine Learning: Trends, Perspectives, and Prospects*. Science, 349(6245), 255-260.
- Marcus, G. (2018). *Rebooting AI: Building Artificial Intelligence We Can Trust*. Pantheon.

Journal Articles

- Agrawal, A., Gans, J., & Goldfarb, A. (2018). *The Economics of Artificial Intelligence: An Agenda*. University of Chicago Press.
- Ransbotham, S., Kiron, D., Gerbert, P., & Reeves, M. (2017). *Reshaping Business with Artificial Intelligence*. MIT Sloan Management Review.
- Chui, M., Manyika, J., & Miremadi, M. (2016). *Where Machines Could Replace Humans;and Where They Can't (Yet)*. McKinsey Quarterly.
- Kaelbling, L. P., Littman, M. L., & Moore, A. W. (1996). *Reinforcement learning: A survey*. Journal of Artificial Intelligence Research, 4, 237-285.
- Tobler, P. N., Fiorillo, C. D., & Schultz, W. (2005). *Adaptive coding of reward value by dopamine neurons*. Science, 307(5715), 1642-1645.

White Papers and Industry Reports

- McKinsey & Company. (2021). *The State of AI in 2021*.

Bibliography

- Deloitte. (2020). *State of AI in the Enterprise, 3rd Edition*.
- PwC. (2019). *AI Predictions 2019: What's Next for Artificial Intelligence?*
- IBM. (2020). *AI for Small Business: A Practical Guide*. IBM Corporation.
- Microsoft. (2020). *AI in Business: How Artificial Intelligence Can Help Your Company*. Microsoft Corporation.
- Google. (2021). *AI Adoption in Business: A Practical Guide to Moving from Pilot to Scale*. Google Cloud.
- Ascend.io. (2021). *AI Implementation: The Roadmap to Leveraging AI in Your Organization*.

Online Articles and Blogs

- Marr, B. (2020). *The 10 Best Examples Of How Companies Use Artificial Intelligence In Practice*. Forbes.
- Chollet, F. (2021). *What is AI?* Towards Data Science.
- Ghosh, A. (2021). *How Small Businesses Are Using AI to Grow?* Entrepreneur.
- U.S. Chamber of Commerce. (2020). *Enhancing Entrepreneurship: AI's Big Impact on Small Business*. Link
- TELUS International. (2020). *50 Beginner AI Terms You Should Know*. Link
- Jetpack. (2020). *AI Trends and Advancements*. Link
- Gridlex. (2020). *Transforming Industries with AI*. Link
- West, C. (2020). *Planning Your Small Business AI Strategy: Key Steps to Consider*. LinkedIn. Link
- MarTech. (2020). *How to Assess Your Organization's AI Readiness with the 5P Framework*. Link
- Multimodal. (2020). *How to Calculate AI ROI*. Link
- TechTarget. (2020). *10 Common Uses for Machine Learning Applications in Business*. Link
- John Snow Labs. (2020). *AI in Healthcare: Customer Stories*. Link
- Harvard Business Review. (2023). *Robots Are Changing the Face of Customer Service*. Link
- Viso.ai. (2020). *Computer Vision in Retail*. Link
- Berkeley CMR. (2024). *The New Data Management Model: Effective Data Management for AI Systems*. Link
- Microsoft. (2020). *AI Skills and Resources*. Link
- Raconteur. (2020). *Four AI Case Studies*. Link
- NCBI. (2022). *AI in Healthcare: An Overview*. Link
- Forbes. (2024). *How AI Tools Can Make More Money for Small Businesses*. Link
- CMSWire. (2020). *AI in Customer Experience: 5 Companies with Tangible Results*. Link
- Webenor Moeyc, P. (2020). *Understanding AI's Impact on Marketing ROI*. LinkedIn. Link
- Element Logic. (2020). *Seven Powerful Uses for AI in Warehouse Operations*. Link
- Homebase. (2020). *AI for Small Business*. Link
- Harvard Business Review. (2019). *Building the AI-Powered Organization*. Link
- BairesDev. (2020). *In-House vs. Outsourcing: Pros and Cons*. Link

Bibliography

- MIT Sloan Management Review. (2020). *What Leaders Should Know About Measuring AI Project Value*. Link
- Cook, J. (2023). *20 AI Tools to Supercharge Your Business and Productivity*. Forbes. Link
- Ronin Consulting. (2020). *AI for Your Business*. Link
- DigitalOcean. (2020). *Open Source AI Platforms*. Link
- OWASP. (2020). *AI Security and Privacy Guide*. Link
- Power, R. (2024). *AI Implementation: 3 Reasons Why Businesses Falter with Integration*. Forbes. Link
- Harvard Business Review. (2018). *How to Get Employees to Stop Worrying and Love AI*. Link
- European Commission. (2020). *Ethics Guidelines for Trustworthy AI*. Link
- Blackett, D. (2020). *AI-Powered Personalization Strategies Driving Small Sales*. LinkedIn. Link
- Harvard Business Review. (2021). *Using AI to Track How Customers Feel in Real-Time*. Link
- Suttmann, P. (2020). *Case Study: How AI Chatbots Transformed Customer Service*. LinkedIn. Link
- Appinventiv. (2020). *AI Sentiment Analysis in Business*. Link
- Akkio. (2020). *AI for Inventory Management*. Link
- Gramener. (2020). *AI in Supply Chain*. Medium. Link
- Harvard Business Review. (2023). *How AI Will Transform Project Management*. Link
- Rhem, T. (2020). *Implementing AI for Maximum ROI: Cost Benefits*. LinkedIn. Link
- Mailmodo. (2020). *AI in Marketing Examples*. Link
- Quantilope. (2020). *Best AI Market Research Tools*. Link
- Scratchpad. (2020). *AI Sales Forecasting*. Link
- Appseconnect. (2020). *AI in E-commerce: 11 Use Cases You Should Know*. Link
- McKinsey & Company. (2023). *The State of AI in 2023: Generative AI's Breakout Year*. Link
- McKinsey & Company. (2018). *Notes from the AI Frontier: Modeling the Impact of AI on the World Economy*. Link
- Harvard Business Review. (2020). *A Practical Guide to Building Ethical AI*. Link
- Abiteq AI. (2020). *AI Small Business Case Studies*. Link
- Warden, P. (2018). *TensorFlow for Machine Intelligence: A Hands-On Introduction to Learning Algorithms*. O'Reilly Media.

Case Studies and Practical Guides

- IBM. (2020). *AI for Small Business: A Practical Guide*. IBM Corporation.
- Microsoft. (2020). *AI in Business: How Artificial Intelligence Can Help Your Company*. Microsoft Corporation.
- Google. (2021). *AI Adoption in Business: A Practical Guide to Moving from Pilot to Scale*. Google Cloud.
- Ascend.io. (2021). *AI Implementation: The Roadmap to Leveraging AI in Your Organization*.
- Ronin Consulting. (2020). *AI for Your Business*.

Bibliography

Educational Resources

- Coursera. (n.d.). *AI for Everyone*. Andrew Ng. Link
- edX. (n.d.). *Artificial Intelligence: Business Strategies and Applications*. UC Berkeley.

Ethical Considerations and AI Governance

- Jobin, A., Ienca, M., & Vayena, E. (2019). *The global landscape of AI ethics guidelines*. Nature Machine Intelligence, 1(9), 389-399.
- Binns, R. (2018). *Fairness in Machine Learning: Lessons from Political Philosophy*. Proceedings of the 2018 Conference on Fairness, Accountability, and Transparency.
- European Commission. (2020). *Ethics Guidelines for Trustworthy AI*. Link

www.ingramcontent.com/pod-product-compliance
Lightning Source LLC
Chambersburg PA
CBHW052331220526
45472CB00001B/361